Children in Community

CHILDREN IN COMMUNITY

SOCIETY OF BROTHERS

Woodcrest, Rifton, New York
Evergreen, Norfolk, Connecticut
Oaklake, Farmington, Pennsylvania

Photography & Art Editor: Roswith Arnold
All photographs were taken in the
Communities of the Society of Brothers.

Library of Congress Number 6319099

Printed by Turnpike Press, Annandale, Va.

Every child is an idea of God. We cannot and should not try to shape a child according to our own intentions. This would be no true service to the child. We should not force on him anything that has not been born into him, awakened from within, or given him completely new by God. God knows what this child is intended for; He has conceived an idea for him from all eternity, and He will hold to it. The service which parents, teachers and community must render the child is to help him become what God's original idea meant him to be. Now it seems hidden, but from day to day, from year to year, we must grasp it with growing clarity. Then we will shape the child not after our own intentions, but in service to the growth which is God's idea for him. That is the secret of the service we should render to our children.

Eberhard Arnold

When we speak of bringing up our children, we mean guiding them. We believe that children lack experience of life and hence of evil as well and need guidance by those who may recognize in time the dangers which threaten a child and stimulate him to struggle against evil. This evil is the craving will which turns from God and acts according to selfish human desires.

Our education starts with trust in the good and genuine things in the child, which, growing alongside other and extremely dangerous forces, finally become predominant and powerful. At bottom it is trust in the voice of God rising in every child as a desire for community and as joy in purity, truth and love. We show this trust in our daily dealings with the children through respect and reverence for the essential good which is alive in all children. In an educational community like ours we must foster the best that is in everyone, especially in the undeveloped soul of the child. For us, education means awakening the child to the essential and ultimate thing that lives in the depth of his heart.

Still, it would be wrong to suppose that there is no struggle in a child's life, no temptation to evil. That insight into the nature of a child which we owe to Jesus only, shows us how terrifying it is when the will to evil appears in a child and urges him on to action. This is why children must be led to arouse and strengthen their own ability to give themselves to the good. The important thing is that they be inwardly occupied with the good, interested in the things of God and filled with the powers of the divine. The free will must not be left unprotected to fall prey to evil. It must be won over to the good. Everything depends on whether we apply this arousing labor of love at the point where the child is really a child.

Educating a child does not mean subjecting him to a harsh nagging, a critical analysis, a ruthless condemnation or a command devoid of faith. It means trusting him, stimulating him and lending him a helping hand. It means seeing the real child-nature in every child. It is this child-nature which continually stimulates the educator and fills him with new strength. Love for the child affirms and intensifies his childlikeness and constantly strengthens it with forces of good, so that the child does not fall victim to an intentionally bad action.

That is the meaning of our education: to lead children to unity, which is God's idea and God's will for men on this earth.

Eberhard Arnold

THE FAMILY

We cannot understand people of our time if young families think it is something regrettable to have to leave other work and to have children. When we receive a beloved child from God a little soul is given to the parents and to mankind. A new little life is given into this world.

For every child the family life is of greatest importance. Modern psychology does not warn us in vain of the serious effects of a broken home, or of a home with a lack of love. Today in the 20th century we know more about the deadly effects in the soul of a child if a child does not find the love of the parents. The Bible speaks seriously to us about reverence and the command to honor father and mother. Only in the atmosphere of reverence before life, only in the atmosphere of respect before the soul of the child, in short only in a truly loving home will the child find the soil to grow in true respect before father and mother.

The fact that the child is often not wanted belongs to a time where love grows cold. The family, the bond between father, mother and children, belongs to the first creation.

The child's being is rooted in the home and in father and mother. If the child grows into a lack of reverence or even into hostility towards father and mother, then the child develops deep-rooted insecurity and unhappiness for his future until he finds reconciliation in love.

Only in Jesus do we find this love, this reverence and this inner security which the child needs. We cannot give any form to our children, just as we like. If we as parents serve the children rightly we accept them as they are, as a great and precious gift from God. Then we strengthen in the child what he is meant to be and fight in the child all that what wants to destroy the soul. If we as parents love God with all our heart and soul then our children will find the right reverence for father and mother. Reverence before the child, the wonderful mystery of being a child and becoming a child, and reverence before the spirit which moves between parents and children is the basic element for a family life, for a true childhood.

Heini Arnold
Thoughts taken from Eberhard Arnold

Little baby in the cradle,
Waiting for the day to dawn,
Sweet little baby,
Sweet as a baby fawn.

Beautiful baby, in a cradle,
As the night is falling in,
Same as the fawn in his ferny bed
Waiting for the night to begin.
                    Dana, age 8

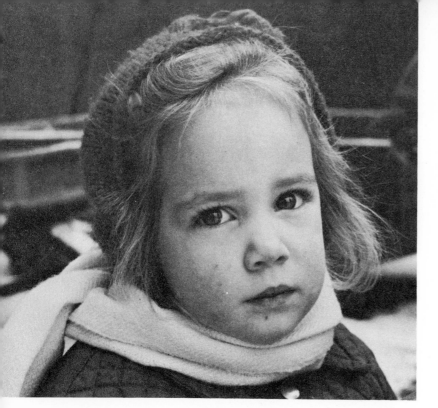

Hilarie

a good read after lunch

She rides her daddy
to the three year old group

and then a nap

10

Home now with big sister Jill

We are ready to go!

Sledding this afternoon?

And it's "family supper" tonight

OUR YOUNGEST

Jesus calls to men to come unto Him as children—that He may lead us to His Father. We feel a deep response to this since we know that each new life is a gift from God entrusted to us as parents. A baby is born knowing only the need of love and food, innocent of fear and hate, and untarnished by the world.

In our care of the young child we carry the responsibility to show him only love. There is in a child the complete trust which so often in the coldness of the world is smothered or broken. We are painfully aware that in our human weakness we can lapse into a coldness of heart. And we see that as we do this we lead a child into inner turmoil which, if severe enough, can even develop into mental illness. Unity and love between parents is vitally important in raising a child into a mentally healthy adult.

The child raised in an atmosphere of real love is more easily led to a life based on faith in God and into a loving relationship to others. Social awareness is apparent at a few weeks as the baby responds to his mother. Even our youngest children spend most of the day in a group with others their own age, and we thus have a unique opportunity to see the joy and response of a young baby to another baby—even at a few months. Babies three or four months old will lie in their cribs smiling at each other; and soon after when put on the floor together will respond to each other in wordless joy. When they learn to crawl, a favorite game is crawling under and between their cribs after one another and peeking at each other from behind the door. One baby at ten months responds to the sound of the names of his group. As he struggles against a snowsuit and winter clothing his mother repeats the names of those in his group—and he quiets down and listens. Another interesting example is seen with babies just under a year who begin to clap their hands as an expression of desire. The teacher begins at mealtime to clap her hands, saying, "Please, more food?" as she gives each baby finger food. Many babies learn within days to clap their hands to request not only food but also toys or being picked up.

We know that true love is not only positive care, but also includes constructive chastening and correction, which are continually necessary. We do not feel that our children are perfect, or are free of possessiveness or

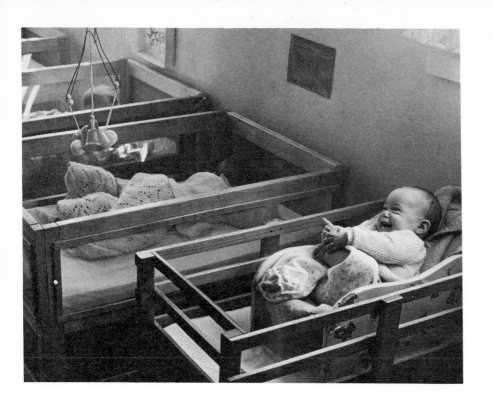

"—please more food."

defensiveness. The age of one year to two years is a tumultuous time. The child cannot articulate his desires, yet he clearly wants independence and adventure. Our children will sometimes retaliate to being hurt and may in turn hurt and bite others. We have not found a satisfactory answer to this in the one year old group except for supervision in the ratio of one teacher to five or six children and physical activity which affords vents for energy.

We find the two year old is really growing up more and more into a responsive, challenging, independent individual. He is beginning to talk in sentences and astounds one by a very advanced phrase sometimes. He also wants to "Do it myself!" in dressing himself, taking off his shoes and socks, putting on his coat and cap. The two year old will help by bringing broom and dustpan, and wiping off the table. The two and three year olds co-operate together putting away blocks on a shelf or small toys in a box. They assume small responsibilities like washing their own hands and faces.

They enter very much into the passing of the year and the many joyful activities of the community—lantern festival, Christmas, winter activities, Easter and the coming of spring, new babies, new families, our pet donkey Eeyore. They feel more and more a part of the whole life and show it by their eagerness and trusting response.

A child surrounded by love and faith will feel the strength of inner clarity and will be nurtured by it. This is a tremendous challenge, for responding to the child's faith in us is the call in our own hearts to respond to the childlikeness of Jesus' message.

Sandy Zimmerman
Loretta Shirky

—two year olds play

—and help

Come out of the house, And in-to the
We're glad you are here, To live — to

air And look at the love-ly world
love And to be with us,

It is for you to live in
To share the world we live in.

Rae, age 9
From the
school magazine, Maple Lane

"Come out — and look at the lovely world."

Children who are too good are certainly a highly unpleasant phenomenon, because their good behavior is unnatural, forced and hypocritical. But naughty children who are unchildlike, presumptuous, disrespectful and impertinent are just as unpleasant. The same thing applies to all egotism, even in the most minor quarrel or in the clamoring for some supposedly marvellous but actually silly possession. And another aspect of this unpleasant evil is the chronic indifference and dull ingratitude which some children foolishly show toward the good and loving things that are provided for them, often at the cost of great sacrifice.

It is important not to get into the habit of being too lenient with the children's moods. Children must learn to take themselves in hand. They must be trained to take a firm and terse stand to what they have done. They must not get the feeling they are ill-used if someone has to speak sharply to them. They must learn to face the music even if it is embarrassing and not give half-answers which could mean this and could mean that. They must learn to speak up with firmness, vigor and assurance.

Obeying comes from listening. If we really listen to what the inner voice of the good and living God says in us, if we learn to listen attentively, then we will learn to obey and follow.

Eberhard Arnold

OUR CHILDREN

BECOME OUR SCHOOL

KINDERGARTEN YEARS

It was a sunny fall day when all the school and as many of the adults who could leave their work for a few minutes lined both sides of the path to the "baby house." The three year olds came trooping out looking solemn and small; as we sang and followed them they made the journey across the community grounds, away from the world of the "baby house," and became the "kindergarten" in the big school house. It was for them a more important moment than they realized; for their parents and those who would spend their school hours with them there came afresh the realization of how delicate a thing it was to help them make the transition from comparative babyhood into ever-increasing responsibility and sensitivity to the world around them. The little troop went through the school house doors and into their new room, scrubbed and shining and lovingly equipped for them. They sat at their new table looking awed and expectant, as we crowded the doorway and peered in the windows wishing them courage in the fight for the childlike and loving spirit.

The next two years of kindergarten, before they enter the grades, are busy ones for the children. There are many new things to learn and many familiar struggles to be continued. A listening ear, a trusting response, a joyful curiosity, an inner respect for others, an open and honest heart go hand in hand with acquiring new skills and new knowledge little by little of the wide world and its people. Which of us does not feel himself weak in all of these? We stand with the children and learn with them and from them. We feel equally cast down and dismal with them when we have to come in from a walk early and have a quiet time because some argued or ran far ahead and broke the joyful unity of the group. Some mornings sing themselves along and we all go home with a bright new picture or a batch of cookies for our families, or a first initial nicely drawn, or a pan of rolls for our shared "Omas" (grandmothers), and a firmer foundation under our feet of joy in being together. Other times are bumpy and we feel raw and edgy, but a new morning or a new afternoon means a fresh start and a small experience in forgiveness on which to build.

It is also for the big school children a good thing to have these little ones there. We seldom have rhythm band but what some older children on their way out to recess peek in to watch us. They come to see what we have in our terrarium. They see the books we share which they too used to love. When the big ones come pelting down the stairs to go to lunch there is a sign in the middle of the hall, "Quiet please, kindergarten sleeping," and one hears them shushing each other before they go out the door. Big sisters and brothers fetch little ones to take them home in the evening. There is a feeling of belonging, of moving forward, of regard for one another.

Before the more serious business of school begins, these two years of kindergarten are a time which can neither be hurried nor prolonged, of free and spontaneous play channeled at times and gradually into more disciplined work. Reading readiness, number concepts, handwriting patterns, all are slowly introduced, but what we long for first is that the children are free to be themselves, loving little individuals, with warm hearts, feeling all about them God's love and protection.

Jane Clement

Time for snack

Kindergarten shares a story

Once upon a time there was a little boy who made a picture with only rain and the wind on it, and that little boy after he made that yellow wind and that purple rain, there was a bang and after that bang there was dynamite. After that a big truck came up the driveway and do you know who was in it? But the little boy, me of course. Stephen was playing with me.

Told by Larry, age 4.

KINDERGARTEN LETTERS:

When David had his fifth birthday his Mommy and Daddy, Kathy and Merrill Mow, were away on a long trip. His kindergarten group celebrated with their teacher, Anneli, and wrote these letters telling about it:

Dear Mommy and Daddy,

Yesterday was my birthday and yesterday I invited Barbara and Arthur and Gary and on Sunday the rest of the group will come. And in the night I always wanted to look in the living room and Emma said I couldn't because I might see a surprise there. Yesterday we went for an all-morning trip to the farmhouse—it was a surprise trip. At snack out there we had a cake. It was chocolate, white and pink. And we had lollipops and I had an orange one. And we had milk with marshmallows in and they tasted yummy. Also at snack we ate in the farmhouse and at dinner we ate outside. And also we went real far in our Reading and Readiness books. Yesterday we made a dam in the stream and made a pool. And then it got deeper and before it had hardly any water and then we let it go. We played with our dollies in the water. I had my bear and he went in the water and then he got all wet and then he was heavy and we put him in the laundry.

Love, David.

Dear Merrill and Kathy,

We saw two "water sallies" (salamanders) and we saw real little tadpoles and we tried to catch them. We played "ship ahoy" up on the porch. Me and David and Xavie found wishing pebbles. And we saw two crabs. And we went under the bridge. On the way back we went a different way. And we didn't ask and we each got a pink sherbet. They had yellow spoons in them. And we dived our dollies off big high cliffs. And a truck came across the bridge. My daddy planted corn and tomatoes in the garden and also beans. In my garden I have gourds and there are two big ones and they are my biggest ones. And the raccoons got a lot of corn today.

Love, Gary.

Dear Kathy and Merrill,

David threw his teddy bear in the water and it made a big splash. And we put him on the rock to dry. The dollies were learning how to swim and dive. David's bear could dive but he couldn't swim because he always sunk. Gary's dollie learned how to make a flip. Our Reading Readiness pencils are all sharp. And I took a wishing pebble and I slept on it and I wished that Tar Baby (a lost cat) would come back and next morning he wasn't home and my mommy said that when it gets cold he'll come home. And she also said that Tar Baby must have paid us a visit while we were asleep. And for breakfast we had cream of wheat. We learned one word in Reading Readiness—it is "Tom," and I told Tom Potts and we always pretend that he is a wolf and he said that we should learn to read "wolf."

Love, Xaverie.

Dear Merrill and Kathy,

At the farmhouse we were swimming and it was real cold water and we saw two crayfish. And when we had dinner two yellow jackets came on our food and we had to put our cups over them and then they flew away. And also at dinner I saw a yellow jacket on my knee. And also it was hot there at the farmhouse. We played up on the porch there at the farmhouse. Anneli was on the porch and we were downstairs on the ground and she dropped marshmallows in our mouths and nobody caughts them 'cept Arthur did. At snack and at dinner we had marshmallows in our milk. And at dinner time there were two marshmallows left over and we gave them to David and one was on top and one was underneath in his cup. And also for dinner we had peaches and peppers and tomatoes and egg sandwiches. On the way home I ate my lollipop. I also had a peach and I ate it at snack time. And nobody asked and we got a surprise with a dairy queen.

Love, Gladys.

THINK ABOUT JESUS

Once there was a big pond and there was a little house with Baby Jesus in. Suddenly a lot of knocks came at the window and that was some poor families. And they lived in a very small house and they had a poor baby, then the wind came and some other poor people had no house and they went walking. And then they suddenly saw a light and then there was Jesus fast asleep, and then he was awake and then Baby Jesus said, "Good morning, have you got a home?" and then the poor people said "No," and then Mary came in and asked Baby Jesus if the poor people had a house and Jesus said "No," and then Mary and Joseph showed them a house with many spare beds. Then God sent a spider and they were very kind to it. Then it was a ladybird and flew away. Then all the poor people said "thank you" to Jesus.

Told by Susan, age 4-1/2

Gary, age 7

a first grader

HOW WE MADE OUR LANTERNS

My lantern was yellow. First we took a piece of paper. I drew round a star on a red piece of paper, cut it out and stuck it on. Many stars I stuck on. Some moons, just one a whole moon. Then I oiled it. It had to dry. We stapled it together. For the bottom we got a paper plate and cut it a little way. We stapled the bottom on.

We need a candle
And a handle.
And then we all went for a long lantern procession.

Taken down from Meg, age 5

*digging is work
and fun*

*Kindergarten plays
with toys made by
their daddies in
the shop*

PRIMARY SCHOOL

To be with children in community is to experience life as a whole, together. Each day, whatever it brings, is a challenge to live in childlike trust and acceptance, in a free spirit of purity and unselfishness—that life with our children might be a truly shared experience.

As we live the daily life we realize that the children, as well as we grown-ups, are imperfect, and time and again we have to struggle for the right spirit among us. But we know we must hold fast to faith that much can be given when love and trust undergird our relationships and daily life.

So much happens in a day, every day, that one is quite at a loss to know where to begin to put down in a few short pages those things that might picture life together.

We start the day in our families and then go to our various groups. The day may be one in which there will be much coming and going—perhaps a family or an individual will be arriving and we want to get a welcome greeting ready: pictures drawn, a "moss garden" made, or even some cookies to put in the room. Or it may be in a special season of the year when there are decorations or presents to be made. We may want to prepare for a celebration, a play or music for some special occasion or for "family meeting" on Sunday morning when the whole community from babies upward meet together. There may have been a new life given and we are going to sing to the new mother and her little baby in the "mother house," where mother, daddy and baby stay a week or so for a quiet, restful time. Or it may be just an ordinary day with school work, noon rest-time, snack time in our families, some kind of afternoon activity like art, games or music lessons—and then the next chapter of *Heidi*, the book we're reading at mealtimes in our group. Whatever the day, we will experience it together.

Those of us who are mothers and teachers have it brought to a sharp focus sometimes how very directly the family life bears on the other experiences. We feel with the whole community the need to find the right way with our children in all we experience together—to try to guide them on the one hand, and yet to be children as they are, weak and inexperienced, but open to help. For this we turn to the brotherhood life itself, where we as members seek the right way and feel that we are a part of the whole life and that with our children we belong together in a deep sense.

Living in community is a seeking together and in this way children and adults stand as one.

Lois Ann Domer

Conversations between Arthur (age 7) and Alice (age 5) after looking at a magazine with pictures of fighting men.

> Arthur: "You know, if I were a king, I'd call all the other kings together and we would have a meeting. And I would tell them to bring me all their guns. Then I would take all the guns and smash them. Just smash them against the wall !"
>
> Alice: "Oh, yes, just smash them against the wall of the castle!"
>
> Arthur: "Of which castle?"
>
> Alice: "Your castle, because you're a king."
>
> Arthur: "Oh, yes, I had forgotten. That's a good idea. That's what I would do. And then they wouldn't fight anymore."

Lucille lost in thou

Ding-dong,
merrily on high!
In heaven the bells are ringing

Drawings by 1st and 2nd grades

Ding-dong,
merrily the sky
is ringing
with angels singing.
Gloria hosanna in excelsis!

THE FIRST GRADE TELLS ABOUT THEIR DAY

In the morning we wake up and wash our faces. Sometimes we wake ourselves up and sometimes "Daddy might give me a bear hug." Sometimes, when my mommy comes to call me, I'm all cosy in my covers and think it isn't time to get up yet. Then there is breakfast at home. Sometimes we might have time for a story or it might be somebody's birthday.

Then the bell rings for school. We see lots of children on the way to school or to the "baby house" and the daddies going down to the shop or to the office. Sometimes we see Eeyore, our donkey, on the lawn or we might hear him braying and we don't see him.

We have our lessons in the morning. But on Saturday we only have a little bit of writing lesson and then we wax and polish our floor and clean our room. At recess we like to play "school."

At snack time with our mommies at home in the afternoon we sometimes have "Eskimo cookies" that we made in our group for our families. Some children have to get someone at the kindergarten or the "baby house" to take home for snack. We have juice or root beer at our snack time sometimes, and we might get invited to another family for snack.

When we go home in the evenings we like to have stories or play. Sometimes on our way home we go to the office or wherever our mommies are and then we go with them to pick up the laundry. We like to do puzzles or color or play with blocks in our families. Sometimes we invite other children to play until it's bedtime. We like to have our daddies read stories when they come home. And sometimes we turn out the lights and light a candle and sing songs before bedtime.

We like Easter time. From the kindergarten up to the grown-ups we all have breakfast in the dining room. Sometimes we find our Easter baskets on top of the house or in a tree.

At Advent the angels sing in the night and leave candies for us. Sometimes at Christmas when we are eating "family supper" we hear jingle bells and Santa comes with candies and fruit and nuts. One time Santa came riding on top of a truckload of Christmas trees for our families. We have

trees in our homes with many pretty things on them and presents underneath.

At Christmas time we see a play at nighttime and we see the manger and the Christ Child. Sometimes it is outside and we get a lighted candle to carry home.

On our birthdays we do special things. We might have a garland of flowers to wear. Sometimes our families go for a drive and stop at the ice cream store. We open our presents at breakfast time on Sunday. We like to invite our whole group to our birthday snack.

Xaverie, age 7

Margie, age 8

After a snow: "Come and see! The whole world this morning looks like a birthday cake! Some places the chocolate is showing through. The footprints are where the candles were."

Becky, age 6

MAY

May is merry
and the flowers are growing in the woods,
let us dance, let us sing
and play jolly games around the maypole
and hear the birds sing in the woods
and listen to the cuckoo cry "cuckoo!"
And listen to the yellow hammer sing
"A little bit of bread and *no* cheese!"
And listen to all the birds in the sky
and play leapfrog down the first bank
and climb trees
and pick flowers
and make garlands
and sing the happiest songs.

Made up by six little girls in the 1st and
2nd grades

THE TURTLE AND THE FOX

Once there was a turtle and he wanted to go for a walk. It was a rainy day. He thought it would not stop raining but it did stop raining. He was far away from home. The turtle started to cry. Just then a fox came along. He said, "I want to hear your nice song." The turtle said, "I was not singing a song." "I heard you singing a song," said the fox. "But I was crying," said the turtle. "If you don't sing I will eat you up." "You can't eat me," said the turtle. "Then I will throw you in the river." "No, no," said the turtle. The fox picked up the turtle and started down to the river. He said, "One two three and here you go." Splash went the turtle. Before the turtle swam away he said, "Thank you," and then he swam away.

Another day a boy came to swim. The turtle went to bite the boy, but he did not care about the turtle biting him. He just went on swimming. When he went home from swimming he was all red from the turtle biting. That was the boy's lesson after all. The turtles lived safely ever after and the boy never dared to go swimming in that lake again.

The End.

Written by Barbara, age 6

A STORY ABOUT

THE LITTLE DOG

Once there was a little dog. He hadn't none daddy and mommy. He wanted to look for a little boy.

He looked in the town for a little boy. And he didn't find none little boy.

And so the little dog walked on to find a little boy. Now first he found a little rabbit. But he thought that isn't a little boy like I'd like one.

And then he found a little pig. But he thought the little pig would be too noisy because he might say "Grumph-grumph."

Then he saw an owl up in a tree. But the owl didn't see him.

Then he found a little hen. But the little hen was in a hurry.

And then it met an armadillo poking out of his hole, who smelled food. And then it did run out to look for food. And then it did run and find a little piece of meat and gobbled it up. And then the little dog did also want some. So he cried a little bit.

Then a little boy heard him, named David. And he peeped behind a tree and saw the little dog crying. So he slowly went to the little dog that it wouldn't frighten him. He said, "Poor doggy." He picked him up and said, "Do you want to stay with me?"

And the little dog said, "YES, I would stay with you!"

And they did be happy together!

Told by Andree, age 8
and Lucille, age 6.

43

THE MIDDLE YEARS

The middle years of school life for our children continue and deepen the experience of growing outward. The children are increasingly interested in others, in finding out how others tick and why they are different. Children of this age say what they think about each other in a very direct way that is not always easy (but often healthy) for their classmates and their teachers. It is a struggle to learn again and again how to live together and accept each other in a loving way.

Children at this age are beginning to be able to do more things: pictures, pottery, writing letters, building models, acting plays, eagerly helping with work projects like the school garden or keeping the skating rink clean. They respond eagerly to the chance to do these things and can work hard for long periods. They wish to play hard too, and a teacher who plays with them will feel their gratefulness.

Gratefulness! Here again it is a struggle for the children to remain really grateful for what they have. And they have a lot, as those of us who grew up with much of it can realize: an atmosphere of love and encouragement, an intimate school group that remains an undivided unit, opportunity to do things together or alone.

One of the greatest thrills is discovering new things in nature and studying to find out more about a new bird one has seen, or realizing suddenly the immensity of the universe, the many suns with their many planets and many moons. "Then why is it that just on this earth there are men! There must be lots of earths with people on them!" is one of the first exclamations.

These children are at the threshold of three or four years of being older school children and they enter into it with great enthusiasm. Sometimes they overreach themselves. Sometimes they fall back into childish silliness or quarreling. But always they are trying very hard to find the right way, to stretch themselves, to learn. And always they are a challenge to the teacher to find the same openness and eagerness that the child expresses.

One of the things that brings ever renewed joy and courage in the work with the children is that in the community parents and teachers are striving towards the same goal. There is a close daily relationship between the children, the parents, and the teachers; in the family and the school the children are part of the whole, the community of all who want to live and fight for the spirit of love to rule in all things.

Irene Hasenberg
Tony Potts

GLITTERING TREES

As we were walking outside
We saw a lot of trees that
Had snow and ice on them.

It looked as if glitter
Had been sprinkled on the trees.

The stream had ice on it
That was just like glass.
And if you were very still
You could see the water
Flowing under the ice.

Evan, age 9

THE SNOW QUEEN

The Snow Queen was very sad. She was thinking about how last year had been. She had given the prettiest snow to the boys and girls, but their mothers and fathers had kept the children in, saying, "You must stay in, for last year you caught bad colds, and we don't want you out again." So the Snow Queen thought it would be as last year. Then an idea came to her. Of course, why hadn't she thought of it before! She would wait till all the families were asleep and she would put just a bit of snow and real warm. Then the children could not catch cold. The fathers and mothers would let the children play. The next night she put just a bit of snow everywhere. When the children woke up there was the snow all around. It looked very beautiful. The children begged their mothers and fathers if they could go out. It was quite warm so their mothers and fathers said they could. The Snow Queen was very happy. But that was long ago! Nowadays we like the Snow Queen to put lots of snow and our mothers and fathers don't mind if we catch cold.

Janie, age 10

GARDENING

In February and March the tomato seeds are planted in the houses. Later on, watermelon, canteloupe, peppers and eggplant are also planted inside. We start planting corn outside the last of April.

We go up to the garden and see the fields are plowed and ready. We get into pairs and Glenn gives each pair some corn seeds. The one with the seeds puts them in their places and the other one packs the dirt on them. It is so interesting watching the baby corn come up.

Early in May we plant beans, squash, cucumbers and melons. Some of the beans are pole beans. We cut long poles for them and make rows of teepees by tying four poles together at the top. It's lots of fun watching the vines make the teepees.

We set tomatoes, peppers and eggplant out about the second or third week in May. Most tomato plants are in peat pots.

As soon as the corn is up we have to pull weeds to help the corn to grow. The weeds like rich soil. The crows are also a big problem. They know where we plant the corn. They find it and eat it. But now we put up lots of shiny tin can lids on a long string and it keeps them away.

Then the tomatoes get blossoms. The blossoms soon drop off and tiny green tomatoes appear. The egg plants get yellow blossoms. Peppers, cucumbers and beans also get blossoms. We soon have a big garden.

We have to weed lots now. Soon the beans and tomatoes are ready to pick. Then the cucumbers are ready to pick. Often we get 3 or 4 bushels of beans and many, many bushels of tomatoes in one day.

It's lots of fun to husk sweet corn. You often find a worm while you are doing it. We cut it out and then bring the corn to the kitchen ready to cook.

One of the nicest things is when the melons are getting ripe. We like to sample them to see if they are ready to take to the cooler.

When the frost comes we pick everything if it's ripe or if it's green. At the end of the harvest our group went up to the melon patch. There were quite a few small melons left and we sampled all of them.

During the summer we set up a stand down on the highway by the Silver Bridge. We are always glad when our turn for selling comes. It is lots of fun. We sell many things and sometimes people give us some extra money. With our money we buy musical instruments for the school orchestra.

Janie and Linda, age 10

"It's lots of fun to husk sweet corn."

"We watch the vines make teepees."

*Experiments in
geometry*

Marion, age 12

Gladys, age 7

Rachel, age 9

We, twelve children and their teacher, roasted marshmallows while the stars shone through the Oak trees.

UPPER SCHOOL

The children in the upper school—the 6th, 7th and 8th grades—are beginning to look toward the time when they leave the community school to attend high school. They look forward to this with eagerness, yet they feel the ground of the children's community still firmly under their feet. These last three years have often been an especially joyful and meaningful time for the children.

This firm ground which they feel is related to their own group experiences as well as to what they experience in their families and in the whole community.

In the group there are often things to be straightened out—a good atmosphere fought for.

"Why did we argue so much at recess?" . . .

"We have to listen to each other, not just to the teachers." . . .

"Let's say what we ourselves did wrong, not what someone else did." . . .

Through many experiences of talking things out freely and openly together, and through hard times and good times, mutual trust and loving regard for each other can grow.

The school group also feels itself very much a part of all that the whole community experiences. Both noon and evening meals are shared with their parents in the community dining room. Here stories of special interest to the children are often read, songs of the seasons learned and sung, or a news report heard. The children often contribute to these mealtimes with music, or perhaps a report on a school activity or trip. Here the larger "family" of the whole community draws together in a joyful and natural way to share whatever the day brings to us.

In arrivals and departures, special meals and celebrations, all that the rhythm of the year brings, the children are in the midst of it—with singing, dancing, music, pictures, and an ever ready joy and enthusiasm.

In the spring, with the coming of Easter and the re-birth of nature, the upper school helps the middle grades with the planting of the garden and the making of maple syrup.

> The winter now draws to a close,
> And now the maple sap—it flows,
> The nights are cold, the days are hot,
> Glenn Swinger I'm sure knows the spot
> To tap a tree on such a day.
> He clears his throat and then does say,
> "How bout we start to tap today?"
> We run get a drill and bore a hole
> Just in the place where Glenn has told us to.
> We put in a spile and hang up a can
> And start a fire and put on a pan
> To boil the sap into syrup.
>
> Steph, age 12
> From "Maple Lane"

They go to the pond for nature study and struggle to finish the schoolwork. "How much longer now till holidays?"

Then the long hot days of summer come, browning teachers and children. The upper school children now help part time in community work, finding experiences in different work departments—kitchen, laundry, baby house, office, shop . . . . The longed-for camping trip really comes, the mountain is explored, the stable for our donkey is built. The garden now is harvested, and some produce sold at the roadside stand (so that musical instruments can be purchased for the school orchestra).

At last the teachers and children sit back after the last "all-day trip":

> The swimming at Kaaterskill now is over,
> The days on the bus have been fun for us all,
> The leaves now are turning, the sky grows more blue,
> And out we must go in the cool bright fall . . .
> Hi-o-o hi-o . . .

The high schoolers go off for the day in town and the community school takes up its work again. The children in the community school always take up classroom work in the fall with real eagerness. In addition to the challenge of preparing themselves academically for high school, they enjoy settling down, stretching their minds to take in new things, disciplining themselves to meet the challenge of the work required. They respect this challenge and do not want to be coddled.

In addition to morning classroom work, the upper school has a science study group meeting in the afternoon, for those specially interested. This year they studied astronomy with a teacher who learned along with them. As a special project they made a map of constellations as they will appear over Woodcrest on Christmas Eve. This map is to be placed in the dining room during the Christmas days so that all may share in it.

In October the whispers start going around: "Soon it's lantern time."—And so it is. This year each child made as many lanterns as possible so that, when the lantern festival came, each person in the community could go out into the darkness carrying a little light. There is something about this festival especially delightful to the heart of a child.

Lorna, age 7

Let us join together
All the lanterns bright,
And shine into the darkness
Like one big glowing light.

Let us wander through the country
With out lanterns burning bright,
Up the hills and down again,
Joyfully singing through the night.

Everyone a lantern bring,
And together let us sing,
Until the world is no more night,
But a big and burning light.

Moneli, age 13

My lantern makes me feel so light;
It takes away the gloomy night.
It shines so brightly that I feel
From dark the light has come so real.

Else, age 12

Shine in my heart, O lantern so bright;
Shine and light up this dark night.
We will follow your soft light
Out of the darkness into the light.

No matter how dark the night may be,
We'll follow your light which all can see.
O lantern so shining, O lantern so bright,
You are my light in this dark night.

Connie, age 13

Mural made by 6th, 7th and 8th grades

As the nights really turn frosty, and the excitement of the first snow is past, there comes the "crowning of the year" with Advent and Christmas time. Long before the Advent angels are heard singing outside the doors, the children are busy with Advent calendars, Christmas stars and secret plans. The request is heard, "Can we write a play to do for Christmas?" Often there are several Christmas plays—by the younger children, the middle grades, the upper school or the high schoolers.

The older school children, aside from all that they experience in community life, are also beginning to see and understand the complexity of world problems and the vastness of world need. To the violence, injustice and suffering which the news brings to them, many respond with shock and protest. Their response is vigorous, for belief in life, in love and justice rises strong from the childlike spirit.

With this comes the youthful urge to work, to go out, to give themselves fully into this need.

Once our older school children wanted to go out to all the farms which we see from our hilltop, to all the country round and tell them about a brotherly life. To the adult mind, problems immediately arise, but to the children it is very simple. They have not lost, and then had to struggle to regain, a belief in the coming Kingdom of God.

Another time we were preparing for a trip to New York by looking at pictures of the city. We came across a picture of a man sleeping on the street under a newspaper.

"Why does he sleep there?"

"He has no home."

"Then we must find him, and bring him home to us."

To live as a teacher with children, one needs to ask over and over again for a humble and a listening heart.

Ruby Moody

Else, age 11

Edith, age 18

CHRISTMAS

POEMS

The earth was still and the wind blew hard,
O'er Bethlehem it sang;
But in the sky a star hung low
For all good men to see.

And then to the shepherds an angel came
And the shepherds were afraid.
The angel told them "To Bethlehem go,
For there a king is born."

To Bethlehem city the shepherds went
To find within a stall
A little boy in swaddling clothes
In a manger he lay.

With animals around him,
Oxen in their stalls.
All the stars in heaven
Shone down upon them all.

Danny, age 12

The pearl that I saw on the
Starry night was so white,
So bright,
So pure;
It glistened out to me.
Then I saw what it was.
It was the Christ Child there.

Carl, age 13

O Jesus child! Your light is so bright,
We praise you so joyously,
And all the angels which round you stand.
We can not keep from showing you
Our love which we owe you.

O Jesus mild! You little lamb,
We come with little gifts to give
To you and Mary mild who laid
You in the manger bed
With ox and donkey at your head!

Else, age 12

One night as winter winds flew fast
Jesus was born to us at last.
Inside a tiny manger he lay
When he was born on Christmas day.

Crowds amassed to see him there,
Angels sang for all to hear.
Many beasts around him lay,
For all were there on Christmas day.

Small and weak he lay abed,
A golden light about his head.
Mary sang to her small babe,
For Christ was born on Christmas day.

Tom, age 12

THE LITTLE MINNOW

A little minnow lay in the bottom of a little pool, sleeping. He was sleeping through the cold months of the year. Suddenly it felt as though the water in the pool was getting warmer. "Is this not strange?" said the little minnow. In the winter the water should be cold and hard. It should be locked in ice. The warmth grew, as if a hot summer sun was beating on it. The minnow shook its fins and paddled to the surface. Here he felt a sort of radiance which seemed to come from above. He stuck his silvery nose out of the water and looked up with his small glassy eyes. He saw to his amazement and wonderment a great light shining down on the little pool. It was a great star. As he watched, a great band of singing, heavenly angels fell from heaven. Of course the little minnow did not know they were angels. The singing and the light filled the whole sky. The little minnow felt something very great was happening. It was. Christ the King was born that night. The minnow flipped his tail and dived to the bottom of the pool. The ripples spread in silvery wrinkles.

Many years passed, and the minnow grew to a fish. But he still remembered that wonderful night. Every year the fish waited for the sudden warmth. Even now he is still waiting, waiting.

Tom, age 12

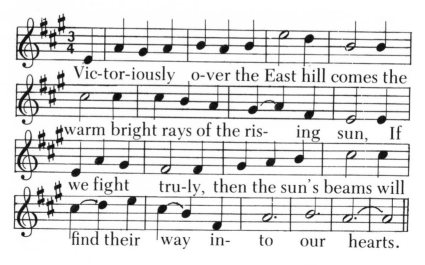

Vic-tor-iously o-ver the East hill comes the warm bright rays of the ris- ing sun, If we fight tru-ly, then the sun's beams will find their way in- to our hearts.

Danny, age 12

A CHRISTMAS STORY

Once upon a time there was a girl called Maria, who lived in Israel near Bethlehem. She was of a poor family and her father was a shepherd. She was the only child in the family because her other brother and sister had died from sickness and lack of food. Her mother was still quite young but looked old and haggard from much worrying and sorrow. Maria loved her father and mother and they loved her very much. They were a happy family besides the fact of little food.

One day her father had gone to the hills to guard a small flock. He had no dinner along as there was no food. Maria waved him good-by from the window and as she saw him go off, without his cloak, she ran out and brought it to him as it was a cold day with a nipping wind. When she brought it to him he said, "Thank you, Maria, but I left it home for you, dear, as you will have to go out and look for something to eat, and it is cold today."

But Maria, noting that her father did not look well, answered, "No, Papa, you need it more than I do, and I can run to keep me warm. Your leg is not quite healed yet and you should keep it warm. Please papa!" she said pleadingly.

"Well," said the shepherd, relenting, "I'll take it along if you really keep yourself warm."

"Oh, of course I will!" Maria answered with a little skip of joy, "and if I find something to eat, I'll bring some to you and Bruno," as she looked at her father's sheep-dog who wagged his tail when he heard his name mentioned. "Good-by Papa."

"Good-by Maria," said her father and waved his shepherd's crook.

Maria ran back to the house to help her mother who was a weaver and weaved scarfs. Her loom was the only important thing in the house which was two rooms. One for the living room, kitchen and bedroom for Maria, and one for a bedroom for her mother and father.

Her mother was at the loom and she looked up as Maria came in. "Maria, could you clean up the mess in the rooms and then go and see if you find some food."

"Oh, yes," answered Maria, "I told Papa that I would bring something for him to eat." She ran and got the broom and started to sweep the floor. After she had swept she cleaned up around, dusting and wiping the tables all the while humming a tune. Then she rolled up the bed mats which were their beds and one ragged blanket that her mother and father used. She used her father's cloak as a blanket.

When she had finished she said, "I'll go now. Good-by."

"Good-by Maria," answered her mother. "Come back if you get cold."

"I will," answered Maria, and ran off to the village Bethlehem.

First she went to the inn, as help was sometimes needed there. In return for food she helped washing the dishes, etc.

She went to the back door and into the kitchen. The Inn Keeper's wife was there and as soon as Maria asked for work in return for food, the Inn Keeper's wife said, "You're just what we needed. I'll give you a loaf of bread if you wash these dishes here." She pointed to a stack of dishes. "We're very busy here because so many people came to pay taxes to the Romans. See you don't get in the way," and she turned to talk to the cook.

Maria went happily to her work, glad at her fortune of getting food. She listened to the maids and lower cooks, some grumbling because of so much work, some talking about how unfair the Romans were, some glad that they might get extra pay for their families. She listened intently, and was surprised when she saw she was done. She went up to the cook and asked if she could have her loaf of bread. The cook was rather cross because someone had spilled a bowl of soup. She grumbled as she went over to where the bread was and picked out the smallest loaf. Maria was disappointed on just getting such a small loaf, but she didn't say anything. It was just enough for one person and it meant she had to work some more.

She went out into the street. No one was in sight except a few poor people because it was so cold.

She went down the street, unsure of what to do next. Then she saw a girl crying by the side of the road. Maria ran to see what was the matter. She was surprised to see how old the child was because from afar she had looked about five years old, but now she saw she was only huddled up and so thin. The girl was about Maria's age. The girl looked up at Maria with big eyes in her small thin face. She had bright yellow hair but it was all tangled. Maria was rather shy but she asked, "What is the matter, and why do you sit in the cold in the street?"

The girl didn't answer but just looked at Maria. She was shivering and it made Maria sorry for her. She took off her ragged shawl and wrapped it around the girl who thanked her with her eyes. She pulled the shawl tighter around her and then, as if she had decided something, she pulled a flower from under her dress. It was a beautiful flower and the girl pushed it into Maria's hand. Maria stared at it wonderingly, and then she cried, "Oh thank you so much! Where did you get it from?"

The girl looked at Maria and then she said, "If you won't tell anyone, I'll tell you. It is quite far from here in the woods in a clearing. There were four flowers like this one, and I picked it."

"Tell me exactly," Maria said, "It's so beautiful."

"Well," the girl said slowly, "you probably know where the woods are and you go up along this street until it turns to go into another road, the one that they sometimes call the robber's road."

Maria shivered, thinking that she wouldn't like to go on it, but she listened further.

"You follow that road," the girl continued, "until you come to the woods where there is a crossroads and you take the road that goes straight into the woods. After you have gone to about the middle of the woods you come to the clearing and in the farthest corner you'll find them."

"Thank you," said Maria, turning to go and then remembered that she didn't know the girl's name.

"What is your name?" she asked.

"Rachel," the girl answered shyly. "Good-by."

Maria then ran down the street not knowing what to do next, when a rich man's cook bumped into her spilling out of his basket two large loaves of bread which fell in the muddy street. The man grumbled and walked on.

Maria happily picked them up and then asked the man if she could have them.

"I don't want them now," the man replied. "You can have them for all I care."

Maria wiped them on her dress and then she remembered the other loaf in her shawl.

She thought, "Oh, I'll just leave the loaf with Rachel. She'll find it and be happy. Anyway I have two more.

She ran all the way home. Her mother had been so tired, she had fallen asleep at the loom. Maria decided to put one of the loaves by her mother and take the other one to her father. Then she remembered the flower which she put in her cup and put it by the loaf. It made it look quite festive. Then she got the blanket and put it carefully around her mother. Her mother woke up then and she saw the loaf and the flower. Maria told of what had happened and her mother carefully picked up the flower.

"Maria, it's beautiful," and her face broke out into one of her seldom smiles. Maria, glad her mother was happy, said, "You can have it."

"Really," said her mother, "Oh, thank you dear."

"I am going to bring the other loaf to Papa now as the field is far off. Good-by Mama."

She ran off to the pasture and was surprised how soon she had gotten there. She had been thinking of so many things. When she got there she quickly found her father who was sitting on a rock stroking Bruno. Her father was very glad to see her and broke the loaf in three pieces and gave Maria and Bruno each a piece.

"You must be hungry," he said to Maria.

Then he noticed that she hadn't her shawl on, but just a thin dress. He asked, "Where is your shawl, Maria?" and he took her under his cloak and on his knee.

Maria sitting there on his knee was warm and comfortable, and she told him about the day's happenings. She went into details and her father listened, asking questions here and there. Both of them were surprised how very dark it was, when they had finished. The night had come fast and now it was quite dark. Her father was worried to send her back and so they decided that Maria would stay with him as he had to stay for the night. Maria went to sleep rolled up in her father's cloak. All of a sudden she was awakened by beautiful music. She looked for her father and saw he was on his knees looking up in the sky. Then she looked up too and saw a host of angels singing:

> Glory to God in the Highest,
> Peace on the earth,
> On the earth be peace
> And goodwill to all
> Who dwell therein. Amen!

She was so awe-struck she just sat there looking up. The sky was filled with a wondrous light.

Then one of the big angels said, "Do not fear, for I bring you good tidings. In Bethlehem a Savior is born and you shall find him in a manger wrapped in swaddling clothes."

When the angels had gone away, the shepherds said to one another, "Let us go to Bethlehem and see the King. We must bring him a gift." And they took their most precious things, lambs, pipes and food.

Maria didn't have anything to bring and she didn't want to come before a king without a gift. She saw her father take his only lamb and carry it tenderly. He was too filled with wonder to remember Maria.

Maria thought about a gift she could give, and then she remembered the flower which the beggar girl had given her. Her first thought was to go home and get it but she remembered her mother's joy of it and how she must like it. Then the thought came to follow the beggar girl's direction to see if there were a few flowers that she could get for the king. Flowers would be just the thing for a baby.

She started to run towards Robber's Road with a little fear, for there had been some awful stories about it. It was shadowed by trees and no light penetrated through the leaves. Then she started on it getting more and more afraid.

Then she remembered the wonderful thing that had happened, angels actually coming to earth and then telling such good news. "Mother would like to know," she thought, "and I will run home as soon as I've seen the King and given him the flowers."

She hadn't been watching where she was going and she stumbled over a root and fell down on the ground getting herself all dirty. She picked herself up, brushing off the main dirt, and went on running. Soon she came to the crossroads and almost took the wrong road because it was so dark. She found out though in time and took the right one and then ran along it. It was pitch dark, and it was getting cold so she ran on stumbling on roots and rocks and getting very tired. She went on in this way till finally she reached the clearing. She found the flowers quite quickly, even though it was so dark, because they were so clear and bright.

She picked two and started on her way back, which was uneventful except once. She heard a twig snap and thinking it might be a robber ran as fast as she could. She soon got to the town at this rate and then she all of a sudden thought,

"Where is the manger?"

Then she saw it, a big, radiant star over where the inn was.

She was somehow drawn to it and went running to it even though she was so hot and tired. She reached the inn and saw that the star was over

The crib Scene

the stable and also two little angels holding candles. Then she looked at her flowers. They had grown quite bedraggled and limp and Maria sadly looked at them. She decided she would at least look through a crack in the door and see what she could see. She went to the door and looked through. There she saw a man and a woman by a manger and in it a baby with such a radiant face and somehow it had light glowing around it. Then she saw her father and the other shepherds kneeling by and then she saw her mother with the happiest face Maria had ever seen. She had her best shawl with her. Then in another corner she saw a little girl she knew who was blind. And look! she was looking all around, she was actually seeing. Maria gasped in wonder. All around the manger were angels singing. Maria looked again at the baby, and then she felt she must go in. So she slipped inside and then remembering she had no gift looked at her flowers. They had grown beautiful again, much, much more than before. Then Maria ran over to the crib and gave the flowers to the baby. He smiled at her and clutched the flowers in his fists and waved them around, throwing light in all the corners.

Maria knelt down beside her father and she was happy, happier than she had ever been and her heart felt full of love for the baby King.

Moneli, age 13

One of the important obligations of education is to give equal valuation to all services and abilities, whether they are physical or mental. As early as possible, we must recognize whether a child is better suited for mental or physical work and what particular kind of job fits his natural abilities. The child will be able to develop his abilities freely only if we combat constantly and from the start the delusion that some kinds of work have a higher status attached to them than others which are just as useful and also serve the common good. A child's personality and the tendencies of his abilities can be observed in his play even at a very early age. Every real child is intensely engrossed in whatever he does. The very way a child sees, the astonished wonderment with which he drinks in the things his gaze rests upon, has in it none of the absent-minded indifference and superficiality of most adults. The inner concentration of his look shows that self-abandonment and self-forgetfulness which we must have if we are to take in what we see in its essential nature with all the hidden meanings clinging to it. The child's play with sand or clay is the primary stage of experience in shaping matter which soon brings gifted children to work of real merit or even artistic value with paper or modeling clay, wood or metal.

Eberhard Arnold

IN EVERY CHILD THERE IS

A LOVE FOR THE EARTH

Every real child lives in nature and with nature. Its living soul is obvious to him wherever he looks. It should not be hard for the educator to bring the child to see creative power at work everywhere. The child should see how all nature is united by the bonds of mutual aid; at the same time he should be brought to realize the dark side of life, the destructive struggle for existence. In every child there is a love for the earth, a joy in the starry universe, a warm interest in the mysteries of atoms and animals; all these things urge the child to awake to love for God and for Christ, the Logos which creates and transforms all things.

And so we rejoice with the children in their joy in nature, in their delight in flowers and forest, in horses, dogs, cows, goats and rabbits, in deer and birds and everything else that lives.

For them, God is not nature itself, nor is He in nature. They find Him above and behind the whole of nature, which is His creation, never in some separate part of this creation.

Eberhard Arnold

"Every child lives with nature"

*We rejoice with
the children—*

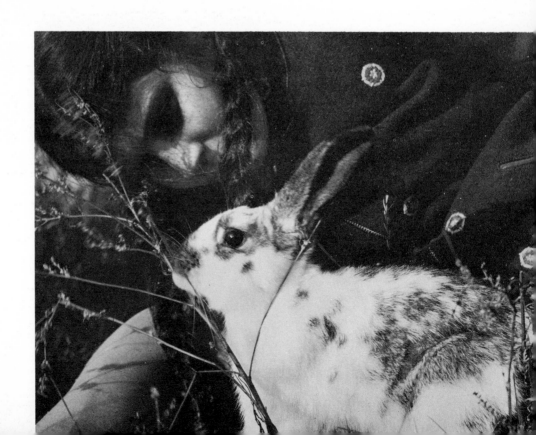

*—in everything
that lives.*

Tommy, age 13

Rachel, age 11

WORK AND PLAY WITH THE CHILDREN

To see and experience children of all ages freely and completely enjoying the out-of-doors in play, study and work is a great thrill and a deep challenge. Our children simply have countless ways and means of doing this. During the summer months there are many different trips: swimming and hiking in the Catskills with some daring mountain climbing perhaps for those who are especially eager and keen; nature walks and hikes to find new plants and flowers that are blooming in the woods with perhaps a little work on the side to construct a fairy village of mushrooms, moss, pebbles and bark which the little children will have the joy of discovering; projects often suggested by the children, to make the dining room extra nice or something extra special for one or the other of the families—these and many other things are constantly happening in our children's community.

I must say that play is a very important part of the lives of our children. Perhaps I say this partly because I would often rather have a roaring game of chain tag with the children than struggle through a difficult lesson on Egyptian history. But when it is possible for children to play together intensively and with all their energies in a harmonious and wholesome way, then it is a very great gift. It is also a struggle for it to be so, for children also must overcome their selfishness and selfwill. We usually play very simple games such as Prisoner's Base or Captain Hook, which are just plain running games and may not look as if they amount to much at first glance. But the children will play these games day after day and by the hour, inventing clever ways to chase and catch, and never tire but will ask again for the same. I am again and again amazed that boys and girls can so freely and unselfconsciously play together, work together and be together.

We have done many work projects in our school groups, sometimes connected with academic studies but mostly to help in some small way the work of the community. The older children, eleven through thirteen, work in some department of the community each day for an hour or more. Boys do dishes from younger children's suppers, carry laundry to various family homes, clean and maintain the school shop and pottery, repair bicycles and sleds,

a roaring game of prisoners base —

take care of the donkey and work with their fathers also. The boys all have a great joy in this work and seldom want to change to a different job when the time comes to switch. Girls help in much the same ways, including the baby house, kindergarten, cleaning the school, the art room and pottery, and tending the school library.

Last year the children had a logging project under way which also had fruitful results. Each week one group of the older children works for an afternoon in the school wood shop. There was very little good wood to work with at the time and we were having a hard time going ahead. It happened

that a large ash tree blew down across the main road near Woodcrest, and we got the idea to cut it into lengths and take it to the sawmill to be sawed into lumber to use in the school shop. That gave all a good time at sawing, hauling, dragging and pulling to get that log ready to go. But it didn't end with that. Another log was obtained which had been lying along the power lines after having been cleared the year before. This one was maple. Then a road-widening in the nearby village provided a large number of cedar logs to be added to the project. Several other trees, either blown down or cut down, provided cherry, walnut and oak to add to our growing stock of logs. All of this work was done with the children together, with many of the children taking chips of cedar or walnut home to show their mothers and fathers.

Then the day came to take the logs to the sawmill. The first trip was made but the sawmill was not operating, so we had to leave the logs to be sawn. But there were more to be taken and all were so eager to see the logs being cut that we arranged for the next logs to go on a day when they were sawing. That was a great day when the children who had worked so hard could watch this final step. They have made very many nice things for their families and for friends from all that wood.

Another project the children have embarked upon this past summer and which is drawing to a close now is the building of a house or barn for our donkey, Eeyore. We didn't have any place to keep him in the winter and many of the children were already worried about his shelter. So one of the men drew up a plan for a stable and the children set to work digging the foundation. It was set in the side of a high bank just off the school play area. This made it necessary that the wall of the stable facing the bank be made of stone so it would not rot out and would be strong enough to support the loft. After digging there was still a hard rock ledge at the back that had to be moved somehow. I as teacher acquired a bit of dynamite and we set to work to dig holes in the rock to blast it loose. Well, I guess that with the first blast there was much more noise than actual rock loosened, but the interest of the entire community was certainly aroused! Eventually the job was managed, and the walls were begun, after the foundations were completed with cement left over from another construction job in the community. The children all worked hard hauling rocks to the site for the building of the wall. Somehow these rocks were all fitted into the wall which rose slowly from one day to the next. Several boys worked on it each

day at work time, and quite a group would work on it one afternoon each week.

Looking finally at the completed wall, several children pointed out special stones which had a real history and meaning to them. "That's the biggest one that took us a whole afternoon to get on the trailer after it fell off once!" —"That one fell off the trailer and smashed my finger."—"This one rolled down the bank and broke the cement foundation." And so it went. And of course all in the community came from time to time to see how it was going forward. After the stone work was finished the wood part went very fast. The walls were soon all completed and the floor was put on. The rafters rose in one afternoon with the boys climbing around on them and securing them in place. Then many hammers went to work to put on the boarding. Children and teachers, working in snow and freezing rain, were seen on and under the roof almost all of one day in an effort to get the building under cover. Then the shingling began and boys worked at all times, volunteering their free time to work on the roof. It was soon weather-tight. Now the stable is almost finished and the children are all looking forward to the moment when Eeyore the donkey can move into his new home. Several of the children remarked one day as we were going to work that this would be a wonderful stable for the baby Jesus to come to and Eeyore could be right there too.

Now in the approach of Advent and the Christmas time I just can't help feeling a real challenge and gratefulness to be able to work with and live with all of our children. The childlike heart of hope, trust, joy and faith has so much to say to all of us and we can never be grateful enough for this in our children.

Dwight Blough

Mural made by 7th and 8th grades

A DROP

I saw a color in the grass,
I saw it swaying and it shined like glass.
I wondered, wondered whatever it could be
and then I saw it was a drop,
It hung from a blade of grass.
The color was the reflection of the sun
And there it hung, that only one.

Marion, age 12

SNOWDROP

A snowdrop white
with green stalk bright,
it bends and sways in
the wild west wind.

The rain pours down
upon his head
while I'm snug and warm
in my nice warm bed.

Oh, poor little thing
I'm so sorry for him.

Suzanne, age 11

Oh, little hepatica,
How did you get so blue?
Under the pine tree
Swaying in the dew.
Did the little blue butterfly
Come and sit with you?
Oh, little hepatica,
How did you get so blue?

Jill, age 10
From "Maple Lane"

I saw some leaves fall from a tree,
They danced across the ground so free,
Then turned around and said with glee,
"We dance today," and laughed at me.

I felt so stupid standing there,
So I ran after them to share
The fun they had
In the autumn air.

Judy, age 12
From "Maple Lane"

YEAR'S END

The trees are bare and black in November,
The wind is swift and strong;
The birds have all flown to the south,
Their nests have been empty long.

The fieldmice will not poke their heads
Above the grasses tall;
And birds will sing their songs no more,
Their sweetest songs of fall.

Still the crows' harsh sounds we hear,
The bluejays scream and call;
But soon they too will be silent,
For snow will cover all.

Joanne, age 13
From "Maple Lane"

MUSIC

Music is an important part of the life of the children's community. From the spontaneous outburst of song when the children start off for a trip in the bus to the combined efforts of the entire school in learning some difficult piece for orchestra or choir, a wide range of music is enjoyed and used in expressing what the children feel.

Almost as soon as the children learn to talk they are singing the simple "Hallelujah" round of which they never tire. And throughout the early years as toddlers and on into the kindergarten years, to sing about what they experience in nature is just as natural as to talk about it. Can't you just imagine them going for a walk in the rain, all donned in their colorful raincoats and hats, splashing in the puddles and singing, "Pit, pit, pat go the little wet feet"? Or singing any of the dozens of early spring songs as they discover the slender green shoots of a crocus, the tiny buds opening on a bush, or a Johnny-Jump-Up in bloom?

For the children in our grade school the summertime with all the trips to the mountains or to swimming places suggests the hiking songs, folk songs of many nationalities, or lovely songs of nature. At the end of the day around the campfire, or on the return trip in the bus, one after the other of many beautiful evening songs are sung.

A very special time for singing is Christmastime when from the first Sunday in Advent until Three Kings Day in January, all ages are singing carols of the birth of the Christ Child. The small ones like to make the rocking motion as they sing,"We will rock you, rock you, rock you." And when they experience the manger scene on Christmas Eve, it is all so real to them as they sing, "To Bethlehem I would go, to Jesus through the snow," "Silent Night," "Away in a Manger" and many others.

Once a week, the children of the grade school meet for "Kinderschaft" This is a coming together as a school and in this time we can sing together old favorites and learn new songs; it is a time of sharing when the children may learn of happenings which have particular significance to them or hear news of children from the other communities.

The children's choir which is made up of the children from the fourth

through the eighth grades gives opportunity for a closer working together. To tackle a difficult round or canon, or to sing in three-part harmony is challenging work, and when the songs are learned it means a great deal to the children to sing as a choir for the entire community at a welcome meal or some special occasion. One song which they particularly like to sing is "Jesu, Joy of Man's Desiring" with several of the older school children accompanying with cello, piano and recorders.

The children from the sixth grade up find it a great joy to sing with the adult choir of the community in learning bigger choral works. The chorus parts from Mendelssohn's "Elijah" and from Handel's "Messiah" have recently been learned and have been combined with either choral reading or a single reader to give the entire story of the work.

Singing together is only one part of the musical picture. The children are encouraged to learn an instrument, usually beginning in the second or third grade when a recorder is received as a very welcome gift. Then group recorder lessons begin through the school program and continue for several years until a basic understanding of note-reading and time is developed. Usually at about the fifth or sixth grade a child will express a desire for training on another instrument—a violin, the piano, cello, a brass instrument, clarinet, or one of the bigger recorders. At this time an effort is made for these lessons to be given.

Meanwhile, all the children from the first through the eighth grades are playing together in the school orchestra. Interest is keen and eyes are alert as each child finds his place for the weekly practice. On the floor in front of the conductor are the first grade children with their rhythm instruments— triangles, bells, drums or sticks. Behind them are three rows of children and teachers in a semi-circle, each one following the beat of the conductor— starting, stopping, repeating, or accepting whatever disciplined learning is necessary. Haydn's "Children's Symphony" is one of our favorite pieces with its bird whistles, and cuckoo and nightingale parts.

The young people attend the local public school and find an opportunity for further training and experience in the high school band. The high-schoolers and some of the older school children join the adults in the community who wish to form a community orchestra. The orchestra usually practices Saturday after lunch in the community dining room. These rehearsals are enthusiastically listened to by the younger children, especially if a mother or father, sister or brother is playing.

In all of our singing and playing together, the important thing is not the quality of the musical performance, although we try to do the best we can with our limited means and talents. The important thing is the spirit in which we give ourselves—to be a unit as an orchestra, to be one voice as a choir.

It has been said, "After silence, music comes closest to expressing the inexpressible." In some moments we experience something of this.

Marlys Swinger
Lois Ann Domer

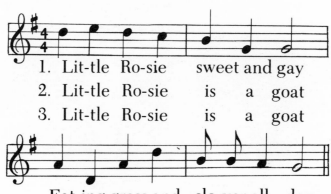

1. Lit-tle Ro-sie sweet and gay
2. Lit-tle Ro-sie is a goat
3. Lit-tle Ro-sie is a goat

Eat-ing grass and clo-ver all day.
She is tied on a long long rope.
She has a fur-ry white and brown coat.

Written by the first grade
after a walk to see the
neighbor's goat.

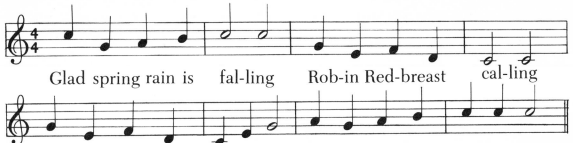

Glad spring rain is fal-ling Rob-in Red-breast cal-ling

Ferns and flo-wers drip-ping green Chil-dren laugh-ing by the stream.

Wendy, age 13

Eeyore's welcome at "family meeting"

Our Children Grow Up

THE HIGH SCHOOLERS

After the children finish the eighth grade in our community school they go out to public school. We are very grateful to the high school for their understanding help and their concern for all the young people who come under their care. This going out has not meant any abrupt change in our children, nor in their relationship to their community home. They meet many challenges in high school and have to find their own way and stand on their own feet. They remain children who are slowly and naturally becoming young adults. They can, if they are determined, remain free from the corrosion of a false social pressure to become "counterfeit adults," and from the forced preoccupation with sex which has spread like a sickness through our American high schools.

One hesitates to speak too much about the great gift of a childlike spirit, which can be lost so early and quickly among teen-agers today. We can be very thankful when adolescent boys and girls are able to be together naturally (working, hiking, swimming, folk dancing, putting on plays) as real friends in unselfconscious comradeship and affection, with mutual respect.

During the summer months, the high school students may work outside the community to get further experience, or they may work in one of the community work departments. At least one day a week is spent on an "all day trip"—for swimming, hiking, or other activities. At the end of the summer the groups have often gone for a camping trip together to the seashore or the mountains.

During the senior year of high school the question of further training is worked out with each student and his parents. Then the community considers together, as any family would, the interests and abilities of the student in light of our limited financial resources. The young people have often won scholarships or worked to help pay for their education. In addition to those studying in liberal arts colleges, we have at present students in training for nursing, elementary education, auto mechanics, agriculture, secretarial work and nursery education.

The wish of the community is not to hold the children at home, but rather to give the uncertain every chance to be away, to see the community life at a distance, to make a free decision as to where and how they wish to give their lives.

Ruby Moody

*High schoolers act Tolstoi's
"What Men Live By"*

Window Transparency made by high school group.

Sexual impurity is the most dangerous poison of untruthfulness and deceit. It robs us of freedom. Any instance of impurity dissolves and destroys the framework of a firm character. Impurity is untruthfulness and disloyality; it is the prime sin against unity among human beings. Purity is the essence of love and, like truth, it is the secret of the life which is God himself. The life of God is love in purity and truth.

The deepest thing we can ask for our children is that while they are still at the innocent age when they cannot yet distinguish between good and evil, the whole atmosphere in which they live may be filled by the Holy Spirit of purity and love. That must be our chief concern, otherwise we shall be guilty of a crime against the children. Secondly, for the children who have reached the age of well-defined concepts and decision between good and evil, we must pray that the spirit of God may act in them, the spirit that rouses the wills of men, so that their wills are made pure, clear and absolute.

Eberhard Arnold

In our fatherliness and motherliness, in our human love, we have been given a natural force for good. It was breathed by God into the first creation. These forces are alive and at work in every human heart and in the heart of every child. They will always be the starting point for a constant labor of soul and mind which, through suffering and seeking and longing, brings people spiritually close to each other. There is some mysterious creative effect in believing in this good; it produces an atmosphere of trust and confiding. Many apparently dead seeds of good can be roused from their paralysis by the warm rays of believing love. These forces are there and we can never thank God enough for them.

But we cannot generate out of ourselves the courage to keep taking up new responsibilities. Even if we throw all the motherliness and fatherliness of our human love into the balance, it is not enough to outweigh the burden of inherited evil. We cannot free men from their lower impulses. We cannot redeem our children.

The new life and the power of the second and different creation which Christ gave us bring a different and greater love, the love of God. It springs fresh from His heart into our hearts, though they belong to an aging and degenerating human race. This different spirit, which is more than all the force of our minds can muster, can make use of us in spite of all our weakness, as soon as we stop confiding in our own strength and the strength of other people, empty ourselves of these delusions, lay ourselves open to Him and hold ourselves always open. For this was the love Jesus made real, and no one, no matter how much he may be in the grip of Christ's spirit, possesses it so inevitably and constantly as Jesus did. This new divine creation brought by the Holy Spirit is more than, and also distinct from, all the natural love of our fatherliness and motherliness. It is the gospel to every living creature.

Eberhard Arnold

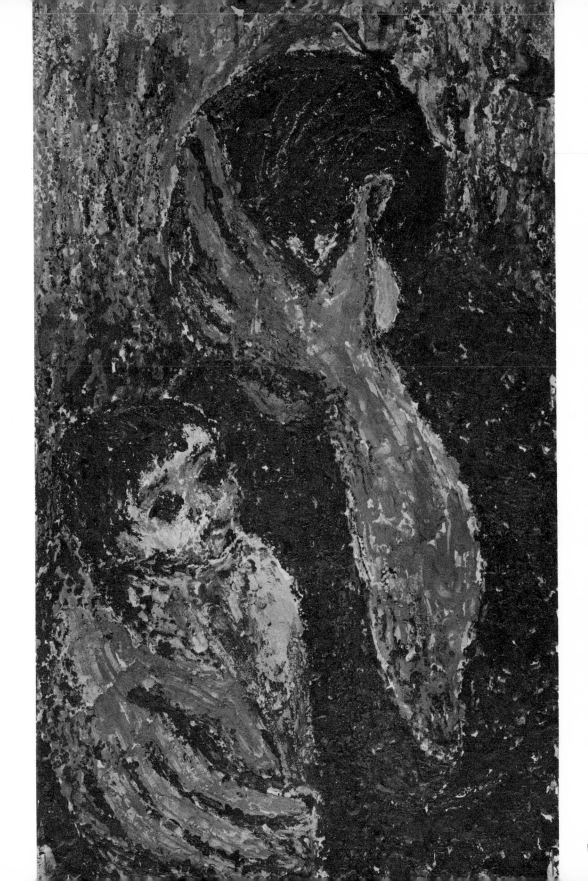

Anna, age 16

Having read this far, many may be interested to hear about the origin of our community, of which the children's community is such an essential part.

After the First World War there arose in Germany the youth movement, which was very much alive in our Christian circles. My husband, Eberhard Arnold, and I were closely connected with this movement for many years. We were part of a group of people who often met in our home in Berlin in a search for a new, genuine way of life. A few of these people felt together the very strong urge to build up a life in truthfulness, simplicity and poverty, as opposed to the life we saw everywhere round about us.

In the year 1920 this community life came into being; a very simple life in complete sharing was begun by a little group in Berlin. This life in community ever and again new born, has continued for nearly 43 years. It has gone through sorrow and struggle, yet through deep joy and real enthusiasm.

Community is a miracle. People cannot remain together for the sake of traditions. Fellowship must be given again and again as a new birth.

Emmy Arnold

Other Publications by the Plough Publishing House

Inner Words for Every Day of the Year, chosen and arranged by Emmy Arnold. Each day brings you a quotation from the writings of both Blumhardts, Dietrich Bonhoeffer, Bodelschwingh, Eberhard Arnold and others. These men were willing to put into daily practice what they believed, regardless of the consequences. 1963. 188 pp. Price $3.00. Cloth bound.

The Secret Flower, a story by Jane T. Clement, taking place in the England of the Middle Ages. This story documents the awakening and groping of one medieval business man toward the land of the "secret flower." 1961. 64 pp. Price $1.25. Paper bound.

Joy in the Lord, a talk given by Christoph Blumhardt on Christmas Eve, 1899, in Bad Boll, Germany. Blumhardt speaks of his longing that men gather together to live for God's kingdom on earth. 1963. 16 pp. Price 30¢.

Christoph Blumhardt and His Message, by R. Lejeune. The first English translation. Tells of Blumhardt's life and gives nineteen talks selected from the hundreds given by Blumhardt in his lifetime from 1842 to 1919 in Moettlingen and Bad Boll, Germany. 1963. 242 pp. Price $3.75. Cloth bound.

The Hour and Its Challenge, by Eberhard Arnold. This pamphlet is concerned with the question of peace. How can man find peace? How much time is yet allowed him? Re-edited 1961. 11 pp. Price 20¢.

The Peace of God, by Eberhard Arnold. This book translates a chapter of "Innenland: A Guide into the Soul of the Bible." Also includes a brief introduction to the author's life and work. 1940. 96 pp. Price $1.50. Paper bound.

The Early Christians, by Eberhard Arnold. The author shares his deep understanding of Christ's followers from the time of the death of the apostles until about 180 A.D. 1939. 124 pp. Price $1.75. Paper bound.

Order from
The Plough Publishing House
Rifton, New York